# THE
# BASICS
# BOOK
*of ISDN*

## SECOND EDITION

## Motorola Codex

**MOTOROLA
UNIVERSITY
PRESS**

ADDISON-WESLEY PUBLISHING COMPANY, INC.
Reading, Massachusetts · Menlo Park, California · New York
Don Mills, Ontario · Wokingham, England · Amsterdam
Bonn · Paris · Milan · Madrid · Sydney
Singapore · Tokyo · Seoul · Taipei
Mexico City · San Juan

Many of the designations used by manufacturers and sellers to distinguish their products are claimed as trademarks. Where those designations appear in this book and Addison-Wesley was aware of a trademark claim, the designations have been printed using initial caps.

The publisher offers discounts on this book when ordered in quantity for special sales. For more information please contact:

Corporate & Professional Publishing Group
Addison-Wesley Publishing Company
Route 128
Reading, Massachusetts 01867

ISBN 0-201-56374-6

1 2 3 4 5 6 7 8 9 10   MW   9594939291

First printing, November, 1991

# MOTOROLA UNIVERSITY PRESS

**The Motorola Codex Basics Book Series**
*The Basics Book of Information Networking*
*The Basics Book of X.25 Packet Switching*
*The Basics Book of ISDN*
*The Basics Book of OSI and Network Management*
*The Basics Book of Frame Relaying*

## WORLD HEADQUARTERS
20 Cabot Boulevard
Mansfield, Massachusetts USA 02048-1193
Tel: (508) 261-4000, Fax: (508) 337-8004

## SELECTED WORLDWIDE LOCATIONS
**Belgium:**
SA Motorola NV, Brussels
    Tel: 32 (2) 718-5411
**Canada:**
Motorola Information Systems, Brampton, Ontario
    Tel: (416) 507-7200
**France:**
Motorola Codex Systemes D'Information, Paris
    Tel: 33(1) 4664-1680
**Germany:**
Motorola GMBH, Darmstadt
    Tel: 49 (6151) 8807-0
**Hong Kong:**
Motorola Asia Ltd., Causeway Bay
    Tel: 852 887-8335
**Ireland:**
Motorola Codex, Dublin
    Tel: 353 (1) 426-711
**Israel:**
Motorola Israel Information Systems Ltd., Tel-Aviv
    Tel: 972 (3) 751-8333
**Japan:**
Nippon Motorola Ltd., Tokyo
    Tel: 81 (3) 3440-3311
**Spain:**
Motorola Codex Spain, Madrid
    Tel: 34 (1) 634-0384
**Sweden:**
Motorola AB Codex Datacommunications Sector, Stockholm
    Tel: 46 (8) 795-9980
**United Kingdom:**
Motorola Codex, Wallington
    Tel: 44 (81) 669-4343
**United States:**
        Eastern Area, Clifton, NJ  Tel: (201) 470-9001
        Southern Area, Dallas, TX  Tel: (214) 690-5221
        Central Area, Schaumburg, IL  Tel: (708) 576-2036
        Western Area, Long Beach, CA  Tel: (310) 421-0086

# PREFACE

This book is designed for datacomm professionals who are curious to know what they need to know about "ISDN," also known as the "Integrated Services Digital Network."

We assume that you know a little — but not a lot! — about data communications. (If you want to brush up on the basics, ask us for the first book in this series: *The Basics Book of Information Networking*.) We also assume that if you live north of Antarctica, you have already heard some of the hype about ISDN, and that you're more than ready for some hard *facts* about this new beast. What is it? What can it do for you? And how soon?

Chapter 1 gives a quick overview of how we communicators got to where we are today, and so is optional reading for those already in the know about the analog phone network. Chapter 2 is wear-your-hip-boots material — we'll go deeper into the theoretical concepts behind ISDN. Chapter 3 explains how the theoretical material in Chapter 2 translates into hardware and software in the real world. Chapter 4 gives you general ideas about assessing your current network, and about how ISDN might fit into that network. And finally, Chapter 5 presents some typical ISDN applications, stressing what's out there today, and what will be out there the day after tomorrow.

# TABLE OF CONTENTS

# Introduction

Imagine a data communications network that provides universal end-to-end connectivity, wholly (or mostly) over digital lines. Imagine that within this architecture, all of today's separate transmission services could be integrated and accessed via a single set of interface standards. And finally, imagine that you could use this network to move data, voice, image, facsimile, etc., either separately or simultaneously, over the same pair of copper wires.

Congratulations: you've just imagined an "integrated services digital network," or ISDN. It probably wasn't even hard to do.

*Building* such a universal network, of course, is a taller order. But in fact, that effort is now under way. Multinational committees of local and national telephone companies, long-distance network carriers, computer and datacomm equipment manufacturers, and software suppliers are meeting regularly to set the standards on which the notion of ISDN depends. At the same time, public and private ISDN services are already emerging around the world. Over the long run, these local services will merge into one network, and ISDN will be a reality.

What's in it for you? That depends in large part on *what* your company communicates, *how* it communicates, *how often* it communicates, and *how much* it communicates. No doubt, you've experienced difficulties with incompatible equipment, protocols, and interfaces, and you've been frustrated by the delays, communication blocks, and expense those incompatibilities have caused. Perhaps you need backup for analog and digital leased lines without a loss of performance, but you don't want the added cost of maintaining redundant links. Perhaps you're exploring ways to cut MIS costs by making better use of your leased lines. Perhaps you'd like network management without sacrificing valuable bandwidth. Perhaps you just need increased transmission capacity over today's local loop.

Or if you're new at this, perhaps we've just succeeded in confusing you. Don't worry; we can set it straight. Codex has been a leader in data communications for more than a quarter-century. Because we have multi-technology experience, we consider ourselves to be networking specialists. We will serve as your guide and partner through the following pages, and help ease the plunge into the (mostly) interesting world of ISDN.

There is no last word on ISDN, and there probably won't be for the foreseeable future. Much of what you'll encounter in the trade press on ISDN — and almost *all* of what you'll read in ISDN-related marketing literature — has that "gee whiz!" tone that makes corporate MIS people clamp a protective hand over their wallets. If you're one of those people, good for you.

We've tried to give this book a very different tone. We don't have stars in our eyes, and our prose isn't purple. Of course, we're as interested as any company in the dazzling prospects of what ISDN *might* be, a few years down the road. In fact, we're leaders in the effort to set the standards and develop the technologies that will make those dreams come true.

But we're very much aware that business decisions begin in the here and now. If your company is like most, you want to make the communications equipment you've already got work harder. And if ISDN can help you do that — if it can increase your flexibility at a competitive cost — you're interested.

You should be, because in many cases, ISDN *can* do those good things.

# WHAT'S OUT THERE TODAY

## OR

*life among the hybrids*

Let's begin at the beginning. As shown in Figure 1 on page 2, in order for two people who are not in the same room to communicate, three things have to be in place: communication devices (computers, terminals, printers, etc.), transmission devices (telephones, modems, multiplexers, etc.), and transmission media (telephone company lines and switches). Sounds simple, doesn't it? I've got equipment; you've got equipment; and there are all kinds of lines out there. So let's swap data. Let's *talk*.

As it turns out, of course, life is more complicated than that. A number of forces have combined to inject confusion into the system, making it more or less difficult to communicate. Two of these forces are competition (the Big C) and evolution (the Big E).

Competition has brought us a wealth of digitally-based equipment, including "data terminal equipment," or DTEs (computers, terminals, etc.), and "data communications equipment," or DCEs (modems, multiplexers, etc.). Most of the devices in both categories are more or less incompatible with each other. That is, their protocols (the methods or procedures that govern the transmission of data between them) are generally proprietary.

Is there any way to overcome this barrier? As far as DTEs are concerned, there isn't. (They're a — ahem — terminal case.) But as far as DCEs are concerned, there *is* a solution in sight. It abbreviates to four letters. Stay tuned.

Evolution, the other Large Force at work, is taking place all across our hypothetical communications link. One hundred years ago, the phone companies settled upon analog devices (which transform sound into "analogous" electrical signals) as the best way of encoding and transmitting the human voice, and over $100 billion have since been invested in this analog network.

**In a conventional analog network, voice and data require separate communications channels.**

Now, as our technologies continue to evolve in new directions, it's clear that there are many communications applications that call for a new kind of network — a "digital" network, based on the binary (or 1/0, or "on-off") code on which

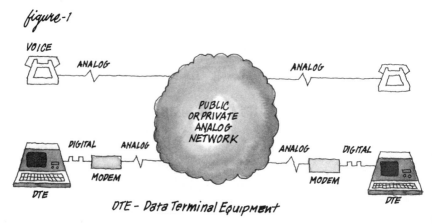

figure-1

DTE - Data Terminal Equipment

computers are based. Not only that, but digital networks are cheaper to build and maintain. Since the 1970s, therefore, the national and international phone companies and long distance providers have been replacing analog devices for switching and transmission with digital devices. At the same time, they've been keeping the interface with the user mainly analog, to maintain compatibility.

There are a *lot* of other good competitive and financial reasons for this shift to digital. Most of them have originated in the workplace, which brings us to the second place where evolution has complicated communication. At work, we still use the phone lines mostly for voice transmission. (In fact, the mix is now something like 90 percent voice, 10 percent data.) But every day, new digitally-based equipment and applications are brought on line. (Personal computers, faxes, video phones: You want it, they'll make it.) It's estimated that by the mid-1990s, half of all communications traffic will be data. We're making new demands on our transmission links, at the same time that most of us are trying to reduce our data transmission costs. How can we put more data through the system, more reliably, with more flexibility, and at a lower cost?

> Today's dial network is used for approximately 90% voice and 10% data transmissions. By the mid-1990s, it's estimated the mix will be 50-50. ISDN is one way to meet this demand efficiently and cost-effectively.

Which leads us back to our opening teaser: life among the hybrids. Today's data transmission networks are hybrids in two senses of the word. First, they're a little bit digital, and a little bit analog. Second, they're a little bit public, and a little bit private.

So what, you ask? Good question. And for dramatic effect, we'll respond with a few other curtain-raising questions:

- Your company is communications-intensive, or else you wouldn't be reading this book. Wouldn't it be great if your company could use bandwidth more efficiently?
- Your company's data communications needs change constantly. Wouldn't it be great if in time you could

tailor your own network to match those changing data-comm needs? If you didn't have to precommit a certain number of channels to a given service?

- Your company may need access to "intelligent" networks, with the kinds of sophisticated signaling capabilities that don't interfere with high-volume data transmission. Wouldn't it be great if the out-of-band signaling capability used within digital telephone networks could also be made available on the local loop? (Did we lose anybody there? Don't worry; it's all in the next chapter.)
- Your company watches the bottom line. Wouldn't it be great if the efficiency and flexibility just described meant that your company could lease fewer lines, and could simply dial up bandwidth if and when it was needed?
- And finally, your company has already made a significant investment in data communications. Wouldn't it be great if all of your existing communications devices were universally "connectable," and could communicate to a network over an integrated interface? Wouldn't it be great if a set of standards could be developed which would create a universal digital network, without making existing networks and equipment — our hapless hybrids — obsolete?

We're betting that you said "yes" to one or more of these questions, and that you're now motivated to slog through some nuts and bolts. On to Chapter 2!

## 2

## ISDN: WHAT AND WHERE IT IS

## OR

*the standards stand revealed*

**OK,** brace yourself for a gaggle of acronyms.

To begin with, you'll recall that in the Introduction we mentioned some of the folks who are working together to define ISDN and ensure that its implementation proceeds smoothly. Chief among these groups is the Comité Consultatif International de Télégraphie et Téléphonie (CCITT), or International Telephone and Telegraph Consultative Committee.

Part of the United Nations, and working with input from various national standards bodies such as the American National Standards Institute (ANSI), the CCITT issues a comprehensive set of telecom standards every four years. These are developed by various working groups focusing on specific standards. (Motorola Codex – your host on this whirlwind tour of ISDN – previously chaired the U.S. working group responsible for the ISDN services and architecture standard and currently participates in many domestic and international standards groups. But more on specific standards shortly.)

The CCITT defines ISDN this way: "A network **evolved** from the telephony integrated digital network that provides **end-end digital connectivity** to support a wide array of **services**, to which users have **access** by a limited set of **standard** multipurpose interfaces."

That's certainly a bit cumbersome, but the key concepts do emerge after a couple of readings. We've taken the liberty of highlighting them in boldface type.

First, evolution, something we already touched on in Chapter 1. ISDN did not come out of the blue. It has evolved logically from the general movement of the telephone network toward digital transmission. That's the macrocosm. In the microcosm — your own communications universe — evolution also plays a role. As you'll see if you read on, there are ways of evolving, or migrating, to ISDN that do not involve replacing your entire network.

Second, end-to-end digital connectivity. In one sense, ISDN is a technology designed to "digitize the last mile" — in other words, to bring the emerging digital network into your office. With it, of course, you also bring all the advantages of digital over analog transmission — speed, accuracy, flexibility, and so on.

Finally, services, access, and standards. These lead us directly to the nuts and bolts of ISDN and so require more detailed explanations (which we're about to embark upon: remember, this is the theory chapter).

**The key idea behind ISDN is to provide *integrated access* to all the services you now have to connect to separately.**

But the key idea is that ISDN uses universal standards to provide *integrated* access to all the services you now have to connect to individually.

Before proceeding, here's a definition of ISDN that puts the key concepts together slightly differently.

(Admittedly, it's longer than the CCITT's, but we think it's also easier to follow): ISDN is an all-digital network that allows users to access a range of today's separate transmission services by means of a single set of interface standards. The goal of ISDN — sometimes called a "switched information pipe" — is to provide universal, end-to-end connectivity, enabling the user to move data, voice, image, facsimile, etc., either separately or simultaneously over the same pair of copper wires. ISDN is part of the evolutionary movement toward digital communications.

Now for a closer look at the what and where.

## SERVICES

We'll begin here because naturally you want to know: "What's in it for *me*?" But if you've turned here first for a sneak preview of how ISDN might change your own universe, you will probably be disappointed. The following section presents "services" as the CCITT defines them. They're, well, *dry*. If you can't wait for full-blooded, ripping yarns about applications, turn to Chapter 5.

As defined by the CCITT, services fall into three categories: Bearer Services, Teleservices, and Supplementary Services. These are summarized in Figure 2.

**In an ISDN network, voice, data, video, facsimile, etc., share one digital link, which provides access to a wide range of services.**

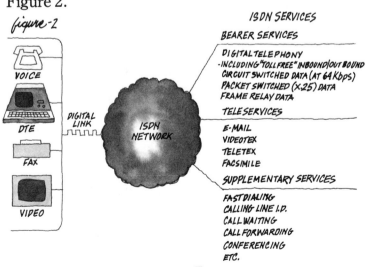

figure-2

VOICE

DTE

FAX

VIDEO

DIGITAL LINK

ISDN NETWORK

ISDN SERVICES

BEARER SERVICES

DIGITAL TELEPHONY
- INCLUDING "TOLL FREE" INBOUND/OUTBOUND
CIRCUIT SWITCHED DATA (AT 64 Kbps)
PACKET SWITCHED (X.25) DATA
FRAME RELAY DATA

TELESERVICES

E-MAIL
VIDEOTEX
TELETEX
FACSIMILE

SUPPLEMENTARY SERVICES

FAST DIALING
CALLING LINE I.D.
CALL WAITING
CALL FORWARDING
CONFERENCING
ETC.

*Bearer services* are essentially what existing analog and digital networks have always specialized in: getting the information from here to there. These are the beast-of-burden functions — including voice and both circuit and packet switched (X.25) data — made faster, more available, and possibly cheaper (please, Mr. Telco!) in the ISDN context. (Frame relay, which is covered in another book in our Basics series, is another ISDN bearer service.)

*Teleservices* are information processing services that are provided to the user via ISDN for a fee. In most cases in the U.S., these cannot legally be provided by the local exchange carrier, but in other countries teleservices may be provided by the national carrier. Such services include E-mail, videotex, teletex, and facsimile store and forward.

*Supplementary services* enhance either bearer services or teleservices. (By definition, supplementary services cannot stand alone.) They comprise most features associated with calls: fast-dialing, calling line I.D., call-waiting, call-forwarding, advice of charges, conferencing, and so on.

## ACCESS

Access, or more correctly, *integrated* access to the above services in an ISDN network is made possible, you'll recall, by "a limited set of standard multipurpose interfaces." To understand what is meant by a "standard interface" it will help to look first at where interfaces occur in the ISDN universe, then at what those interfaces are, and finally at the standards themselves.

## THE BOUNDARIES IN THE ISDN UNIVERSE

The CCITT identifies a number of specific functions encountered in ISDN, and in Figure 3 we've located these functions on our communications link. These functions are:

- Terminal Equipment 2 (TE2), which represents non-ISDN compatible devices (big universe here: analog phones, PCs, terminals, computers, statistical multiplexers, X.25 PADs, etc., etc.);

- Terminal adapter (TA), which provides ISDN compatibility to non-ISDN devices;
- Terminal Equipment 1 (TE1), which represents ISDN-compatible terminal equipment;
- NT2, which includes switching and concentration of ISDN lines on the user premises ("your office");
- NT1, which serves as the customer-end termination of the local phone company's wires, known in the trade as the "local loop";
- LT, the line termination function in the central office of the phone company; and
- ET, the extraterrestrial function. (Weren't nodding off, were you?) Actually, ET represents the switching exchange termination function, again located in the central office of the phone company.

Note that most of the action (TE1, TE2, NT1, NT2, and TA) is on the user's end. Only the LT, ET, and switching functions — the phone company's domain — are outside of the user's direct sphere of influence (although in many countries the NT1 will still be owned by the phone company). In a sense, that's the point.

**CCITT-defined ISDN functions show that most activity occurs on the user end (customer premises), giving you more control over your network.**

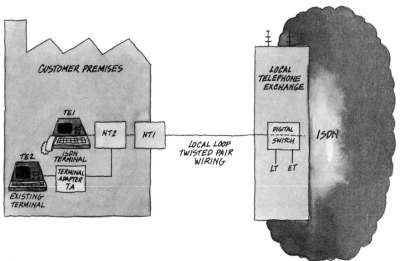

*If and when ISDN reaches its glorious potential, you'll have a lot of control over what you use and how you use it.* You'll be able to go to practically any vendor, purchase equipment capable of performing these functions, and rest assured that it will all work together!

## INTERFACES: WHERE STANDARDS TEND TO HIDE

The CCITT has also defined a series of interfaces between these functional groups. These interfaces are an important conceptual building block in the ISDN network. Logically, if you wanted to maximize flexibility and competition for all the communications functions just described, you'd identify all the points across that communications link where two functions come together. At each of those interfaces, you'd establish universal standards.

This is exactly what the CCITT has been doing.

**For many of the interfaces shown below, the CCITT has established a universal set of standards which ensure CPE compatibility.**

We will look first at the five interfaces the CCITT has identified, and then at the standards established for each of those interfaces. But keep in mind what all this means: that customer premises equipment (CPE) performing like functions will ultimately be compatible — regardless of vendor.

*figure 4*

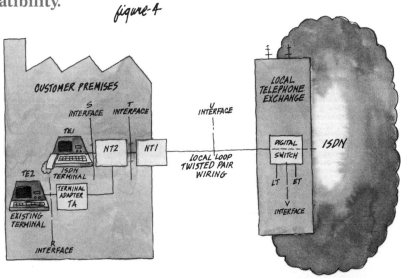

10

The *"R" interface,* as the illustration suggests, sits between a non-ISDN compatible device and a terminal adapter (TA). This is the point between those DTEs that don't support ISDN standards and the ISDN world. There are, of course, many standards for the "R" interface — too many, in fact, and some of them are proprietary — but by definition, they aren't ISDN standards.

The *"S" interfaces* are those points where communication paths feed into an NT2, or customer switching device. This allows use of a single standard interface for traffic originating either from non-ISDN compatible devices (via the "R" interface and TAs), or directly from ISDN-compatible devices.

The "S" interface and the *"T" interface* — the next interface we encounter as we stroll outward from the user to the phone network — are electrically identical. (In practical terms, this means that any device that can connect at one of these interfaces can also connect at the other.) They play a very different role in communications, though.

While the "S" interface carries calls between devices on the customer premises, the "T" interface carries information to and from the ISDN world. Once your message gets out to the "T" interface and an NT1 — the network termination function — it's *gone,* off for care and handling by the phone company. By the same logic, anything that comes down the pipe from the "T" interface is a message from Out There.

An NT2, or customer switching device, can switch voice and data traffic presented to it on the "S" interfaces locally, without going out into the phone network. Or it can switch calls between the public network and the internal private lines. For example: Your PBX, if you have an ISDN-compatible one, is an NT2. It allows you to route your communications traffic internally, without the aid of the phone company, or connect it with the outside world.

Well, we'll have to fudge those last few paragraphs just a little bit in order to introduce the *"U" interface.*

Truth is, the status of your NT1 — which connects to the "U" interface — depends on where you sit in the world. In Europe, for example, the NT1 is owned by the carrier, whereas in the U.S., it is owned by the customer. Discretion being the better part of valor, the CCITT has decided to allow national standards bodies to set rules for the "U" interface on a country-by-country basis.

There is one other tale of suspense and intrigue that arises at the "U" interface. It's known to crime buffs and computer jocks as "The Mystery of the Wire Count," or, "The Case of the Twisted Pairs." To make a long story short, the local phone company's network that arrives at your doorstep consists of a single pair of twisted copper wires (the "twisted pair"). On your side of the doorstep — in other words, on the customer side of the NT1 — the traffic is carried by *two* pairs of copper wires. The transition from one twisted pair to two pairs to connect your calls to the world occurs in the NT1.

The use of four wires at the "S" and "T" interfaces and only two at the local-loop "U" interface grows out of both how we use the phone network and how the phone companies keep their costs down. You, the user, don't care if it's two or two hundred wires poking through the walls; you simply want the telephone connection to arrive alive and well at your premises. And once it's there, you want the luxury of loading it down with multiple devices: telephones, terminals, fax machines, and so on.

At the same time, the telephone company wants to avoid lavishing too much copper or plastic on any one customer. Consequently, a method was developed for creating a "local loop" (connecting your premises and the local central office) that uses the existing two wires. But the method used to connect your office to the phone company won't allow multiple devices to be connected. This multipoint connection requires four wires to work. Hence the need for the NT1 and the two-to-four-wire conversion. And since it's there anyway, it is called into service for a number of safety, diagnostic, and maintenance functions as well. Actually, we've lied a little bit here; the S and T interfaces actually contain eight wires: four for communication and four for various powering options.

Two wires, four wires; so what? Well, in the analog environment, the phone company's two wires can support only one "channel" — that is, they have to give themselves over entirely to a single voice or a single data transmission. In an ISDN setting, by contrast, the phone company's same two wires can be divided into several distinct "channels," thereby making much more bandwidth available to the user. We'll return to this notion of "channels" shortly. (And, inescapably, we'll show how in some cases there are two twisted pairs on *both* sides of the NT1 interface!)

And finally, we present the *"V"* *interface*. This sits deep inside your local phone company, separating the line termination function (LT) and the switching exchange termination function (ET). Think of it as one of those strange creatures that live near the hot vents on the ocean floor, far from the reach of sunlight.

Having thus picked on the hapless "V" interface, we'll end this section with a caution. Keep in mind that these are *conceptual* points — creations of a group of like-minded CCITT participants who want to make ISDN work. The functions that these interfaces are designed to help define aren't necessarily located in a given place (your office, the ocean floor, or separate independent devices). Someday, many of them may wind up in one box. Or, perhaps, on one chip.

## STANDARDS

We communicators have always had standards. In the past, though, we've tended to keep them to ourselves. Computer makers and phone companies (just to name a few) have traditionally tried to establish proprietary standards that their competitors couldn't decode or mimic. Up to a point,

> In an analog environment, the phone company's two-wire loop supports only one voice or low-speed data transmission. With ISDN in place, this can be divided into several "channels", providing more bandwidth to the user.

this is good business: "If you want to get on my network, you have to buy my product."

We are now moving beyond that point. ISDN will incorporate a set of universal and open standards. This will be good news for would-be manufacturers of DCEs and related equipment, since when those standards are in place, anybody who can make an ISDN terminal adapter, telephone, or NT1 can also be assured that it will be 100 percent compatible with the ISDN network. It's also good news for users, who (someday, though not immediately) will be able to purchase a fancy new ISDN phone at the local QuikTechShak in Paris, Texas, and plug it into the wall in Paris, France, with no problem.

Basically, ISDN is about transmitting voice, data, image, or whatever (user traffic). Through the CCITT's efforts, two major transmission rates have been established. Get ready for ISDN Crucial Acronyms Numbers One and Two: "BRI," which stands for Basic Rate Interface, and "PRI," which stands for Primary Rate Interface. (If you expect to hold your own at ISDN cocktail parties, you'll have to memorize at least "BRI" and "PRI.") We start by looking at BRI, since it is polite enough to respect all those interfaces we've just outlined.

Remember when we hinted earlier that in an ISDN environment, you might be able to decrease the number of connections between your company and your local phone company? And that the phone companies were switching to a digital network in part to pack more voice and data traffic into existing lines? Well, here's where it starts to happen. To accomplish transmission at the Basic Rate, the phone company divides its existing Twisted Pair local loop into three separate channels: two 64-kilobit-per-second "B" channels, and one 16-Kbps "D" channel, or "2B+D." The B channels always carry user traffic; signaling information is always carried on the D channel, which may also carry low-speed packet data — but more on that later.

**ISDN Basic rate "B" channels always carry user traffic. Signaling information is always carried on the 16-Kbps "D" channel, which may also carry low-speed packet data.**

On to Crucial Acronym Number Two: PRI, or Primary Rate Interface. In the U.S., Canada, and Japan, PRI consists of 23 64-Kbps "B" channels and one 64-Kbps "D" channel, or "23B + D." In Europe PRI consists of 30B + D. PRI necessitates two Twisted Pairs on each side of the NT1, and is electrically identical to today's T1/E1 services. With PRI at hand, users can move their data mountains at 1.536 million bits-per-second, or something like 150 times what a single telephone currently accommodates. (Europeans using PRI move mountains at 1.920 Mbps.)

Digging one step deeper, and thickening our alphabet porridge, we need to mention that the channels in a PRI can get even bigger. These are called "H" channels. An "$H_0$" channel, for example, is the equivalent of six 64 Kbps B channels, or 384 Kbps. Even larger bandwidth is available when you use the entire PRI less the D channel. In the U.S., this is labeled an "$H_{10}$," and provides a transmission rate of 1472 Kbps, while in Europe, this same beast is called an "$H_{12}$," and runs at a rate of 1920 Kbps. Finally maybe, the U.S. makes the entire PRI — 1536 Kbps — available, and calls

**Basic Rate Interface or BRI consists of two 64-Kbps "B" channels and one 16-Kbps "D" channel (2B + D). PRI (23B + D) provides for 23 B channels (U.S., Canada, and Japan) or 30 B channels (Europe) and one 64-Kbps D channel.**

*figure 5*

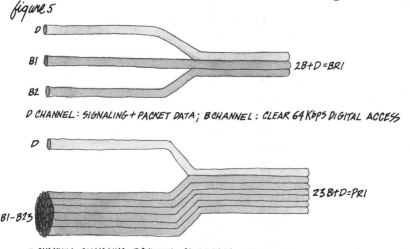

D CHANNEL: SIGNALING + PACKET DATA; B CHANNEL: CLEAR 64 Kbps DIGITAL ACCESS

D CHANNEL: SIGNALING; B CHANNEL: CLEAR 64 Kbps DIGITAL ACCESS.

it $H_{11}$. In this configuration the signaling in another PRI is used.

So far, we've talked about the phone company's obligations and perspectives — that is, life on the other side of the "U" interface. But the ISDN user, too, has his or her own standards to live up to. Remember the "R" interface, on one side of which you've got a bunch of non-ISDN compatibles cranking out the traffic. Obviously, you've got to convert these traffic streams to ISDN-compatible formats, and "package" those streams to use all this wonderful new bandwidth effectively.

Most of us old-fashioned telephone users are more dependent than we know on devices that connect at the "R" interface, since we have to make this leap to get our analog voices out into the increasingly digital telephone network. This is accomplished today by a technique called "Pulse Code Modulation," or **PCM**, which digitizes voice when it's carried over digital circuits between the carriers' switches. When ISDN arrives in full force, PCM will become even more important. At that point, our voice signals will be converted within the ISDN telephone into a 64 Kbps bit stream using PCM. It will then be carried over the ISDN network in a B channel. We'll have no problem talking with Aunt Eileen in St. Louis, even though we use ISDN phones and she still uses an analog phone, because her local central office will perform the conversion automatically just as it does today. (More on Aunt Eileen shortly.)

**If you have an ISDN phone, you can talk to Aunt Eileen in St. Louis even though she still uses an analog phone because her local central office performs the conversion automatically.**

So much for voice. When it comes to data, conversion is accomplished by "rate adaption," a translation task performed by a terminal adapter (TA). To make a long story short, the TA does whatever it has to do to make your data ISDN-compatible. For example, it converts your terminal's electrical interface to that required for ISDN. If you have asynchronous signals, it converts them to synchronous signals. In most cases, it boosts your signal speed to 64 Kbps (the B channel rate, remember?). And finally, it uses the D channel — stay tuned! — to help set up calls and synchronize users' machines on both ends of a communications link.

Depending on the types of equipment you've got, the TA shoots for one of four CCITT standards — V.110, V.120, X.30, or X.31 — or else passes 64 Kbps traffic through undisturbed. Do you have "V" series terminals around the shop? (That's RS232, for our U.S. readers.) If so, then to create an ISDN environment, you'd have to have TAs capable of converting their output using either V.110 or V.120. If you have "X" series terminals, you'd need to convert using X.30, which is similar to V.110 for X-series terminals. And finally, X.31 could be used for either V-or X-series terminals, since it helps them communicate via X.25 over ISDN networks.

The following four paragraphs should be read only for extra credit — or if you plan on attending a truly high-level ISDN cocktail party. The rate-adaption standards just described also suggest ways to combine, or "multiplex," separate data streams on one "B" channel. Multiplexing allows you to use the bandwidth of one B channel to carry multiple data streams and take full advantage of your ISDN transmission capacity.

Two types of multiplexing need to be reviewed. First, "time division multiplexing," or TDM, assigns each bit of data a specific and fixed portion of your total bandwidth. The alternative — STDM, or statistical time division multiplexing — allocates bandwidth based on the amount of data presented by the various connections established over the communications link. It does so by assembling a group of data into a "packet" (or "frame"), and then transmitting that packet along with an address to the other end of the link. If no packets are sent, the bandwidth is available for use by other communicators.

STDM is both slower and faster than TDM. Because it introduces small but variable delays into the transmission process, it is generally unsuitable for some data communications protocols and voice transmission. On the other hand, it can interconnect devices with greater total speed than TDM, because bandwidth is used only when there is data to communicate.

This is interesting only for two reasons. First, it helps us distinguish between the V.110/X.30 and V.120 standards. Simply put, V.120 includes provisions for STDM, and V.110/X.30 does not. Second, V.120 will some-day use a new ISDN service called "frame relay." Frame relay will resemble the current X.25 packet switching networks, but will allow much higher throughput and shorter delays. We will return to the prospect of frame relay in Chapter 5. In that context, we promise, it will be more fun.

## LIFE ON THE D CHANNEL: SIGNALING (and more)

Notice that up to this point, we've finessed this "D" channel stuff entirely. True, we've explained how the B channels in BRI squeeze more bandwidth out of existing lines; and how as a result, they increase total transmission capacity and allow faster rates of transmission. But to hardboiled old data communicators, this is only more of the same. (A lot more of the same.)

It is life on the D channel that really distinguishes ISDN from other digital alternatives to the analog network. The D channel adds new capabilities, the most important of which involve *signaling*. In brief, signaling in the D channel tells the network what to do with the stuff that's being tucked into the B channels. It also makes possible all the supplementary services (Figure 2 again) and provides the user with call control information such as calling line I.D. and billing data.

Signaling, of course, already goes on all the time throughout the phone network. Signaling is what opens and closes switches, routes calls, and so on. Signaling is how switches talk to each other. It's the sophistication and universality of the ISDN signaling function that will, in large part, determine whether ISDN will succeed or fail.

Currently, the carriers with digital networks accomplish their signaling over a separate and dedicated network, outside of the normal communications channel. This is known as common channel or "out-of-band" signaling, accomplished through the transmission of messages (as opposed to simple tones). It allows them to set up calls much more quickly than in the past, leading to better use of existing channels. It also allows them to exchange other information, such as billing data, while the call is in progress.

By contrast, the local loop provided from your local exchange/office uses *in-band* signaling — by all accounts, a clunkier technology. Signals are often tone-based (bip, beep, boop), and must "compete" with your voice or your data for air time. And because of this and other limitations inherent in analog technology, there are limits on the services that the (local) carriers can offer to their customers.

Let's construct a worst-case scenario to illustrate the problem. You're working at home on the high-profile Data Manipulation project, downloading gigabytes of data from headquarters via your modem. The report is due tomorrow. You're anxious. You're a Type A personality, so of course you've installed call-waiting on your home phone. Right in the middle of the crucial data transmission, your Aunt

Out-of-band signaling offers a much more efficient use of bandwidth than in-band signaling.

*figure-6*

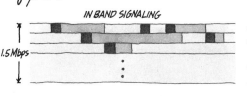

IN BAND SIGNALING

1.5 Mbps

- INEFFICIENT.
- NO SIGNALING POSSIBLE DURING CALL E.G. CALL FORWARDING, WAITING, BILLING.
- EVEN BUSY SIGNALS TIE UP A CHANNEL.

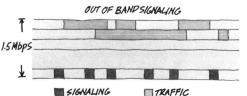

OUT OF BAND SIGNALING

1.5 MbpS

- GREATER EFFICIENCY.
- SIGNALING POSSIBLE WHILE CALL IS ACTIVE.
- BUSY SIGNALS ETC., DON'T TIE UP CHANNELS.

■ SIGNALING    ▢ TRAFFIC

Eileen — remember her? — calls from St. Louis. Call-waiting does its job (bip, beep, boop), putting tones right in the middle of your data. Hello Aunt Eileen, goodbye data. You contemplate early retirement.

With ISDN in place, you can talk to the boss while the data is being transferred, and when Aunt Eileen's call setup message comes through on the D channel, you'll be able to see who's calling. She'll then be put on hold until a B channel is available. Her signal, like all other signaling to and from the (local) phone company on the D channel, will observe the CCITT's "Q.931" standard. It will arrive in the form of information "frames" that conform to the CCITT's "LAP-D" data-link standard. For the first time, and in insider's jargon, you'll be able to get "out-of-band signaling on the local loop." And, if all goes well, you'll have lots more services to choose from as a result.

> With ISDN in place, you can talk to the boss while data is being transferred — and if Aunt Eileen calls, you'll be able to tell who's calling and put her on hold until a B channel is available.

Meanwhile, back on the network, we have one last standard to trot out. This is the switch-to-switch signaling standard, or "SS#7." SS#7 is a monument to teamwork, since this one standard (first issued by the CCITT in 1980, and revised regularly ever since) attempts to define the entire architecture of inter-switch signaling worldwide. It is actually not one standard, but a family of standards, governing such diverse topics as message transfer protocols, structure of the special "signaling network", error and overload recovery, and call-related services in the ISDN universe. Again, out-of-band signaling is what makes most of ISDN's unique services possible. Without SS#7, there could be little life on the D channel.

You're probably wondering by now why the folks at the CCITT provided so much bandwidth on the D channel — a full 16 Kbps for BRI subscribers. Signaling requires only a proportion of this capacity. Rather than waste the remaining bandwidth, ISDN allows it to be access X.25 packet networks for low-speed data applications.

In practice, "packet on the D" allows a 2B + D (BRI) user to make three or more calls simultaneously — two using the B channels (perhaps one voice and one data call to other ISDN subscribers), plus one or more X.25 sessions to users on the packet network. And all this via a single pair of wires connected to the local telephone exchange! (To digress further on this topic would be to write another book. Fortunately, we've already done that. If you'd like to know more about X.25 networking and its many benefits, just ask for our *Basics Book of X.25 Packet Switching.*)

Well, that's the theory. Now for two mercifully short chapters. In Chapter 3, we'll take a brief look at where various types of hardware and software come into play to make ISDN work across our communications link. (Plus, while you're not looking, we'll sneak in a little Chapter 2 review.) Chapter 4 is designed to help MIS managers and other communications professionals assess what they have today, and whether ISDN represents an improvement.

That's the whole point, right?

## 3

## ISDN: PRODUCTS AND EQUIPMENT OR

*naked hardware*

In the beginning —
on the left side of Figure 7, labeled "A" —
there was a dumb terminal.

Or perhaps there was a personal
computer. In any case, if there is to be a
communication, there needs to be a device
to allow for a user application. In the pre-
ISDN world, this piece of data terminal
equipment was in most cases tied into either a dial
modem or leased-line modem, where its digital signals
would modulate an analog carrier, so they could be transferred over the analog telephone network. A 4800 bps
modem, for example, would modulate the analog signal
with the 4800 bps data and send it over the phone lines,
thereby controlling the data rate across the analog
network. On the other end, another modem would

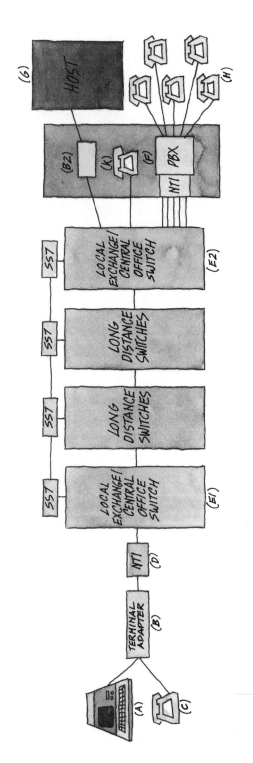

figure-7

24

demodulate the signal, making it digital again to be comprehensible to some other device — perhaps a host computer ("G").

Enter ISDN. Now we have a terminal adapter ("B"), a player already introduced in the last chapter. The TA does all kinds of good things. First, it converts the physical and electrical interface that comes out of the DTE into an ISDN-specific physical and electrical interface. Second, it performs rate adaption, taking the 4800 bps data stream out of the DTE, and — by stuffing it into data patterns according to V.110/X.30, V.120, or other ISDN standards — boosts that signal up to the 64 Kbps rate set by the network for transmission over an ISDN B channel. Alternatively, the TA could take that 4800 bps data stream and "packetize" it into X.25 packets. These packets would then be shoved out on a Basic Rate D channel at 16 Kbps, or a Basic Rate or Primary Rate B channel at 64 Kbps, sent down to the packet handler (an electronic function within the central office switch, not some guy in a postal uniform), and whisked out over X.25 networks to the other end of the link.

**An ISDN terminal adapter performs functions ranging from rate adaption to X.25 packetization.**

Note the little telephone ("C") sitting near the TA. This represents an existing analog phone, which is plugged into the TA. Again, the TA converts the phone's analog signal into a 64 Kbps digital signal (using PCM, remember?). It also converts any signals it receives from the phone's keypad into messages that go onto the D channel. This allows the digitized analog voice signal to be switched by the ISDN public network, and Aunt Eileen's telephone rings in St. Louis.

The interface between the DTE and the TA, as well as the one between the analog phone and the TA, are R interfaces (you'll recall). In many work environments, this could be quite a crowded neighborhood. In other words, there could be quite a pile of DTEs over there at "A," particularly if a Codex TDM or STDM multiplexer were sitting there alongside the TA, helping the TA take full advantage of the available bandwidth. If your equipment is accustomed to 4800 bps, many of those devices could communicate over one B channel (with a little help from your friends here at Codex.)

The terminal adapter, in our diagram, is connected across a U interface to the local office of the telephone company ("E1"). We need to step across the internal wiring/local loop divide with the help of a little box called an NT1 ("D").

When we reach the central office, we need to find a switch that's capable of dealing with ISDN. More than half of the phone lines in use today still use analog switches; if these are to cope with ISDN, they have to have a box of hardware (called an "adjunct") added on to them. Even the digital switches in use today won't jump up and perform ISDN on cue, since they have analog line cards in them. In order for these switches to go to ISDN, they have to have ISDN-based, U interface line cards installed in them. (We're cheating a little bit here, since in fact, numerous other hardware and software changes have to happen here to allow the introduction of ISDN.)

Next, we have the connection between local and long distance networks. In ISDN, all of these circuits have to be digital. In fact, most local to long distance circuits are already digital, as are most connections between long distance networks. As mentioned earlier, the conversion from analog to digital lines has been occurring independent of ISDN, since digital equipment is cheaper, faster, smaller, and more reliable than analog equipment.

Also ongoing, and also independent of ISDN, is the installation of SS#7, a separate network of packet switches, computers, and associated software. SS#7 ties switches together — controlling call routing, setup, release, and so on — and otherwise routes messages related to a call *independent* of the switches that actually carry the call. SS#7 is a prerequisite for an ISDN call between one switch and another, since that's where the (vital, crucial, critical) D channel information is carried.

On the right side of the diagram, we step down from a second local office ("E2") into a variety of customer premises equipment (CPE). For example, there might be five PRI links between the local C.O. and a PBX ("F"). The first of these would provide 23 B channels between the local switch and the PBX (23B + D, right?). The second through the fifth PRI links (actually, there could be up to 20 PRIs) might provide 24 B channels each, all controlled by the D channel in the first PRI. Naturally, we've tied some ISDN phones ("H") into this PBX, in order to take full advantage of the features of ISDN (and to make our diagram more comprehensive).

Sitting as it does between the S and T interfaces, the PBX is an NT2. (Remember that calls on the S interface can be switched locally; calls on the T interface always go out to the central office.) The NT1s can be standalone boxes, or they can be built right into the PBX. In the latter case, the standards people like to think of "virtual" T interfaces, buried away in the bowels of the PBX.

Similarly, the phone at location "K" could be either an ISDN or non-ISDN phone. If an ISDN telephone, it could use a U-interface, BRI connection directly to the local central office (in the U.S.), or it could use a T interface to an NT1. If an analog telephone, it could be tied into an analog line card in the same central office.

Last but not least, another terminal adaptor ("B2"). While depicted as a stand-alone unit in our diagram, this TA could ultimately be built right into the host computer ("G"), have lots of "virtual" interfaces (R,S,T), and carry traffic at B or H channel rates. Alternatively, it could be (greatly) assisted by a Codex stat mux, quietly working to keep your installed base useful in the emerging (but still hybrid) world of ISDN.

# ASKING THE TOUGH QUESTIONS

## OR

*I still detect nebulousness*

Now that you've made some sense out of ISDN, and tracked its footprints across a network, you may want to consider the big question that most of this book has been leading up to: "Does ISDN make sense for me?" And believe it or not, you've already got most of the information you need to decide whether or not to get involved in ISDN. That's because the answer to this question mostly comes from an assessment of the communication capabilities you've already got. How well is your network serving you today? Based on what you can predict about your future datacomm needs, how well will it serve you in the future? What advantages (or disadvantages) would the ISDN alternative present to you?

Let's look at six key criteria:

**1. Connectivity:** At the beginning of this book, we referred to the delays, communication blocks, expense, and other headaches caused by incompatible equipment, protocols, and interfaces. Slowly but surely, the universal and open standards of ISDN will eliminate some of these obstacles and frustrations.

Some, not all. ISDN will not make incompatible devices compatible. Rather the terminal adaptor makes a non-ISDN device compatible with the ISDN *network*. Neither does it eliminate the protocol issues: someone who only speaks Chinese is not going to understand someone who only speaks Swedish even if they're speaking across an ISDN network.

What ISDN does do is to simplify the process of ensuring that only like devices try to communicate in the first place. That is, through SS#7 and the D channel they signal to each other across the network during the call setup phase to make sure both devices are speaking the same "language" — be it 4800 bps, V.120 rate adaption, or whatever. If no device is available to speak that language, the call fails.

> Through SS#7 and the D channel, ISDN devices signal to each other across the network to make sure both devices are speaking the same "language" — 4800 bps, V.120 rate adaption, or whatever — before the call is connected.

The question becomes, then, how much would you be willing to pay to ensure that *every* outpost of your far-flung business empire achieves this degree of connectivity with every other outpost?

Of course, connectivity also intersects with cost (see below). Simply put, can your existing and indispensable equipment really handle the ISDN potential? If you're really married to your hardware, and if that hardware can't pump data out any faster than 9600 bps, then you have only limited use for a 64Kbps B channel.

**2. Availability:** This is equally important, and easier to quantify. Is the capacity there when you need it? In terms of today, what happens at peak-load time? In terms of tomorrow, how fast is your data flow growing? Will the capacity be there tomorrow? (A sleek, well fed, and unavailable network is not optimal.) How much would you be willing to pay for significant amounts of extra bandwidth on demand?

**3. Cost:** OK, let's imagine the capacity is there. What does it cost to *feed* this rough beast, a.k.a. your existing network? Is it efficient, relative to your other options? If you've built to accommodate peak load, are you paying for a lot of unused capacity the rest of the time — that is, most of the time?

One basic problem in running these numbers is that until recently, the most important number of all — the ISDN tariff — has been missing in most locales. Buying into ISDN without knowing what the carriers are going to *charge* you for that service is a little bit like signing a blank check. On the other hand, the carriers (among other players) have an increasingly large financial stake in ISDN. How are they going to play the game?

Experience with tariffs published to date (early 1991) suggests that ISDN voice calls will be tariffed pretty much as they are now. Data calls, on the other hand, look to be considerably less, because you're getting lots of additional bandwidth (64 Kbps vs. 9.6 Kbps) for your money. Access charges — the fixed component in these direct costs — will almost certainly vary widely among carriers, but these represent only a small portion of the total cost of using an ISDN network.

You have to look to the indirect costs to get a full, clear picture of how ISDN is going to look on your bottom line. Benefits such as shorter time to connect (which increases productivity), calling line I.D. (which makes customer data immediately available, as we'll see in the next chapter),

> You have to look to indirect costs — shorter connect time, calling line I.D., portability, manageability, etc. — to get a full, clear picture of how ISDN will look on your bottom line.

portability (which saves you money when you rearrange offices), and manageability (coming up) are all issues to be considered.

It's a safe bet, then, that as a general rule, the overall cost benefits will make ISDN attractive for at least some applications, perhaps including yours.

**4. Flexibility:** Can you push your network around, and make it do what you want it to do? Or do you feel a little bit like the lion-tamer who has to keep the beast up on the stool? Going back to the services listed in Figure 2, how many of those services would you like to be able to access on demand? With ISDN, you can access some of those services today (we'll get to some examples in Chapter 5); others over time. (How much time? Well, there's no definite timetable. Some industries are on a faster track than others. Some countries are on a faster track than others. The point is to recognize that it's out there, it's real, it's happening. And if you do decide that ISDN offers — today or tomorrow — real advantages for your network, you need to have some migration strategies in place. More on these at the end of this book.)

**5. Manageability:** OK, maybe you feel secure on this score; you can manage your datacomm equipment to your satisfaction. But look beyond that narrow focus. When one of your data transmissions hits a snag today, you get no information from your carrier. ISDN, on the other hand, through its out-of-band signaling on the D channel, provides information on call failures, billing statistics, and, in the future, maybe even performance statistics. In fact, with ISDN in place, managing the entire network will be a whole lot easier.

**6. International effectiveness:** No one needs to be told again about the globalization of business. Are you spanning the continents with confidence? As the ISDN sun rises, are you confident about your ability to compete in tomorrow's world? ISDN promises clearer calls right around the globe with rapid call setup and teardown. Moreover, common standards mean dial flexibility, with up to 64 Kbps bandwidth per B channel (and

1.92 Mbps per $H_{12}$ channel) to speed your worldwide data transmissions.

## PUTTING ISDN IN THE RIGHT PERSPECTIVE — YOURS

Get ready for an unexpected turn of events: total candor. If you're confident that your current network is internally and externally compatible; that it's accessible and available; and that it's cost-effective, flexible, manageable, and internationally effective; and that it will continue to be all of these good things for the foreseeable future, then *don't* leap into ISDN.

The fact is, ISDN as it is now being implemented will not be all things to all people. Even the high-speed PRI (23B + D) won't be as fast as many of the LANs (local area networks, for all you decoders out there) now in operation. (And as your LAN is converted to fiber optic technology, hefty rates of 150 Mbps and higher become conceivable. Yikes!) Even PRI won't be suitable for those gee-whiz ISDN applications you may be so tired of hearing about — for example, full-color and full-motion videoconferencing. *Those* applications will only become possible when "Broadband" ISDN becomes available.

**ISDN is not some universal panacea to all communications problems: for example, many LANs are faster. And applications such as full-color and full-motion videoconferencing won't be possible until Broadband ISDN becomes available.**

On that happy day, transmission rates will jump to over 150 Mbps — perhaps as high as 600 Mbps! — and your voice, data, and image will race simultaneously along fiber optic cables — gee whiz! But at the outset, we promised we wouldn't be ISDN cheerleaders; so enough of this Broadband daydreaming.

In short, if things look great right now, be generous. Pat yourself on the back, breathe a sigh of relief, and lend this book to a friend who's in rougher shape. But also recognize that ISDN is a fast-moving target. It's certainly not a safe strategy to lean back in your recliner and hold out for Broadband ISDN at the turn of the century. Every time an ISDN tariff is established or revised, for example, you may want to refigure your calculations.

So keep your finger on that ISDN pulse. If you need help, team up with a company that specializes in networking. (We know of an excellent one.) And read on in Chapter 5 to see how your universe might change for the better in the near future.

# 5

## ISDN APPLICATIONS OR

*I see distinctly now!*

In the following pages, we sketch out three near-term, real-world ISDN applications, indicating in general terms the "migration strategies" used by the companies in our examples. (See the final section in this booklet for more on migration strategies.) If you've been reading ISDN marketing literature — poor soul! — you probably won't find these the most glamorous examples of ISDN's glorious potential you've ever encountered. But again, we've tried to stick to applications that 1) are built on services that are available now, or will be shortly; and 2) might actually have something to do with what your company does today.

On the other hand, they're fun, as well as informative, so think of them as your reward for plowing through Chapter 2.

## 1. Telemarketing without Tears

The Couchpotato Video Market (CVM), a home-shopper cable service, has a problem — it's too success-ful. Home viewers of the CVM station call the CVM free phone number to take advantage of CVM's great shopping bargains. At first, CVM leased lots of "toll free" lines and hired operators to accommodate peak traffic, but the company's managers decided not to pay for this extra capacity in off-peak hours, and scaled back. The new approach is cheaper, but has many limitations.

For example: callers dial up CVM in response to a particularly good bargain. The first lucky few callers get through. Operators take their name, address, phone number, credit card number, and order. Since all interaction is verbal and all information obtained is hand-keyed in, numerous errors are introduced into CVM's data banks. In the course of the call, a credit authorization is obtained from the credit card company, usually taking another 15 to 20 seconds.

Those would-be customers who *don't* get through either get a busy signal or hear a taped message: "All our operators are busy; please stay on the line, and your order will be taken by the first available operator." Based on the number of callers who hang up every day, CVM's managers know they're losing many potential sales through this arrangement. At least *some* people who get busy signals don't call back; and at least *some* people who get put on hold give up long before CVM's harried operators get to them.

CVM decides to go ISDN. This basically involves modifying the software in the company's computer to access customer records based on the "calling-line identification" presented with the incoming call request, and routing that information to the operator's terminal as the operator receives the call.

Today, with ISDN and calling-line I.D. in place, the identity of the lucky few callers who get through is known to the operator before he or she picks up the phone.

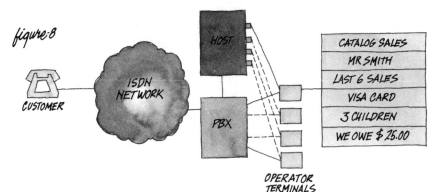

figure·8

CUSTOMER

ISDN NETWORK

HOST

PBX

OPERATOR TERMINALS

CATALOG SALES
MR SMITH
LAST 6 SALES
VISA CARD
3 CHILDREN
WE OWE $25.00

The caller's file is instantly on-screen, enabling the operator to say, "Good evening, Mr. Smith. We haven't heard from you since last August. What would you like to order tonight?" Keystroking is now limited to the order itself, thereby minimizing operator errors and reducing the time required to handle each call. Thanks to ISDN's faster connect times, the time needed for Mr. Smith's credit authorization check has been reduced from 15 seconds to 5 seconds. Mr. Smith, for his part, is pleasantly surprised to receive this personalized, prompt, and accurate service from CVM (which hasn't had the greatest reputation for service in the past!).

**Calling line I.D., one of many ISDN services, increases productivity by enabling a terminal operator to see a caller's identity and to initiate action even before the call is answered.**

Meanwhile, those callers who don't get through are also handled differently with the help of ISDN. A limited number of people are put on hold, to be picked up in sequence as operators become available. The rest hear a new recording: "Thanks for calling CVM. We'll call you back as soon as an operator is free." (Eventually, CVM intends to personalize these messages: "Thanks for calling CVM, Mr. Jones.") The computer's new "number-capturing" feature not only makes such call-backs possible, but also will lead over time to a major expansion of CVM's data base and mailing lists — an increasingly valuable revenue source for CVM.

CVM's story is imaginary, but it's not unreal. Today, a major credit-card company is using such a system on a PRI, and estimates that it has reduced its time-per-call by 17 percent. More calls are being processed and fewer errors are being introduced. Customers seem satisfied with the company's improved services, and the company likes the lower cost-per-call.

## 2. Soft LANdings

The Competent Computer Care Co. (CCCC) has offices in three cities: Canton, Ohio; Camden, New Jersey; and Cupertino, California. Each office is equipped with a local area network (LAN) that interconnects all workstations.

Internal communications within each LAN are simple, but interoffice links are more complicated. Currently, CCCC — which passes a *lot* of data traffic from office to office, including electronic mail, file transfers, and so on — has allocated a fixed portion of the T1 leased-line bandwidth between offices to interconnecting LANs. (An X.25 packet network proved unable to keep up with the data flow.) The remaining bandwidth is allocated for voice traffic between PBXs.

**Before ISDN, Competent Computer Care Company had to reserve a portion of its costly leased-line T1 bandwidth for interconnecting LANs.**

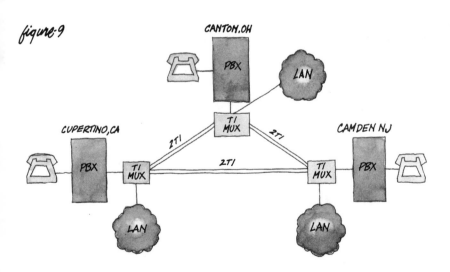

figure-9

This arrangement is perfectly adequate, but the T1s are expensive, and, due to the "bursty" nature of CCCC's traffic and the rigid allocation of the bandwidth, often sit idle. CCCC has experimented in the past with devices that set up calls between separate LANs, but the results have been unsatisfactory. These experiments involved the use of dial modems, which set up temporary links between LANs. But setting up these links took up to 20 seconds and capacity was limited to 9600 bps. CCCC's network managers are in rebellion as a result, and the company has continued to look for new solutions.

**With ISDN, CCCC is able to access more bandwidth as needed via less costly PRI dial connections. This improves connectivity between LANs while reducing line costs.**

The solution that CCCC hits upon is to replace the T1 multiplexers with "nodes" that automatically allocate T1 bandwidth based on traffic load, and that access more bandwidth via PRI dial connections as needed. In this way, CCCC need only lease T1 lines for the base-traffic load; the company can then augment those lines with dial connections when necessary.

*figure-10*

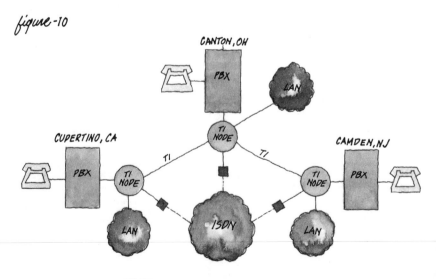

■ *PRI DIAL CONNECTIONS*

An additional benefit of the new nodes is that they support the frame relay access protocol. As we indicated in Chapter 2, frame relay is an ISDN bearer service similar to X.25 packet switching, but it can handle much faster data streams with lower delay than X.25 (see below). It is also "transparent" to all kinds of traffic — meaning that CCCC can connect its LAN bridges into data ports on the new nodes and not be concerned about conflicts.

Now, when someone in Canton wants to send a message to the Cupertino office, the local LAN bridge routes it to the Canton node, which automatically allocates bandwidth to carry the message to the Cupertino destination. If more bandwidth or backup lines are needed, the node automatically acquires it. But note that now both voice and data traffic share the same bandwidth, rather than being separated. This results in a more constant load, and means that there are fewer overflows to dial.

CCCC has been able to improve connectivity between the LANs in its offices while actually reducing its line costs — and all without having to replace its existing PBXs or LANs. As an added bonus, it has enhanced security against leased line failure, with the bandwidth-on-demand available through ISDN.

---

**FRAME RELAY IN BRIEF**
Frame relay refers to the technique of passing "frames" or blocks of information across a digital network interface, using an address applied to each frame to distinguish logical channels. At the edges of the network, the address identifies the traffic source and ultimate destination. Routing is controlled on an end-to-end basis by the network, but link-to-link error correction and retransmissions are not performed. Instead, data integrity is guaranteed by higher level protocols at each end of the network. (For example, X.25 can be used for this purpose.) In effect, frame relay allows data traffic to move along the network "highway", passing through green and yellow lights only–with no red lights to stop it in its path. As a result, it offers very low throughput delays, and supports data transmission in millions of bits per second.

# 3. "PUBLATE" and "PRIVIC:" Homogenizing Networks

The Rigid Antisubmarine Manufacturing Co. (RAM) has an extensive private network with network "nodes" in six cities: Tokyo, New York, Paris, London, Dallas, and Los Angeles. Data and voice lines enter the RAM network at each of these nodes through PBXs. RAM has divided its network into eastern and western segments, with Dallas and New York as members of both segments. The nodes are connected with leased lines between the four nodes within each segment.

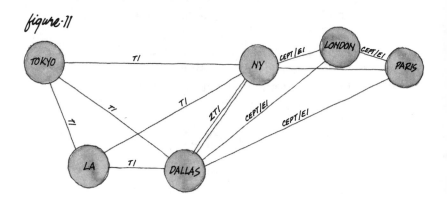

figure-11

Before ISDN, Rigid Antisubmarine Manufacturing relied on many expensive, private T1/E1 links to connect all key nodes in its network.

The system has been planned to accommodate (nearly) peak traffic at all times in all directions. This provides adequate bandwidth and redundancy, but is expensive: most of the time, the leased lines are only lightly loaded. RAM sees no good alternative to this system, though, in part because for security reasons, it is reluctant to resort to dial connections.

One constant source of aggravation for RAM arises when people attempt to direct-dial inward to the various PBXs. Currently, callers have to dial a main number, speak with an operator, and then get connected through to the correct extension. (Several PBXs have installed two-stage dialing, which represents a slight improvement.) But would-be FAX-ers within RAM are grumbling, since the manual setups needed are time-consuming and error-prone.

After a careful investigation, RAM decides to go ISDN. First, the company reconfigures its system of direct links. Instead of leased lines between every node in a segment, RAM analyzes its traffic and eliminates the leased lines which aren't economical. In place of those lines, it sets up a switched service over ISDN. New ISDN hardware and software are installed all across the system.

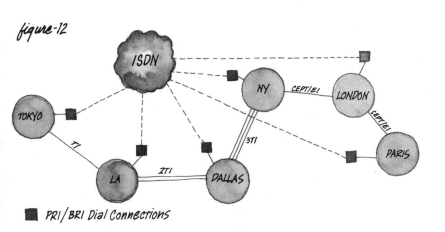

figure-12

■ PRI/BRI Dial Connections

After the reconfiguration, New York and Los Angeles (for example) communicate over leased T1 circuits via Dallas. When these 1.5 Mbps lines begin to be overloaded, RAM's nodes automatically dial up additional BRI or PRI links directly between the end points as necessary. In a real sense, the public network is used to supplement the private network, both for additional bandwidth and for redundancy in the case of leased line failure. The private network is adjusted constantly to reflect changes in traffic and tariffs.

**With ISDN, RAM uses less expensive PRI/BRI dial connections to link some locations and to relieve T1 overloading elsewhere: in effect, the public network is used to supplement the private network.**

Second, two-stage dialing is a thing of the past, since ISDN permits "subaddressing". When managers in RAM's Stuttgart sales office (which doesn't generate enough traffic to warrant a leased line) make their monthly report to the corporate computer in L.A., they use the public network to call Paris, where the call enters the private network. Stuttgart's call not only includes the Paris number as its address and the L.A. computer port in the subaddress, but other parameters as well. For example, Stuttgart's call setup message may say, "I need an asynchronous, 9600 bps, V.110 rate-adapted connection; I can't cope with network independent timing; but I can negotiate rate."

Meanwhile, out in L.A., the Stuttgart signal hits the local node. In the bad old days, pre-ISDN, L.A. supported 24 lines: six running at 1200 bps, six at 2400, six at 4800, and six at 9600. If Stuttgart called looking for a 9600 line and all six were occupied, Stuttgart was out of luck. Today, post-ISDN, L.A. only supports 10 lines — but they can be adapted automatically in response to incoming signals. Stuttgart signals; a computer port is instantly reconfigured from 4800 bps V.120 to 9600 bps V.110; and the call goes through. With fewer than half as many lines, L.A. provides a more available service.

Meanwhile, back in Germany, an unprincipled competitor attempts to dial in to the Paris node for a look-see. Paris, programmed to admit only certain callers into the RAM private network by using calling-line I.D., turns back the threat. Another (small) victory for ISDN!

# 6

## AFTERWORD

*A few words about Motorola Codex*

By now, you've certainly gotten the sense that we at Motorola Codex are interested in making ISDN work for you. At the same time, we're *not* interested in promoting the use of ISDN where it's impractical, unnecessarily redundant, or too costly.

We are convinced that ISDN is not going to arrive all at once. (Babies, as it turns out, don't come from storks.) As noted earlier, we communicators are living in a period of analog and digital "hybrid" networks, and we will be for quite some time. Just to complicate things, most medium- to large-sized companies have all kinds of incompatible DCEs around the shop, representing a large fixed investment. The trick, then, is to master this hybrid environment, with flexible solutions that run end-runs around the boundaries of protocols, transmission media, and so on.

We're also convinced that in many cases, ISDN can and should be added to a "backbone" corporate network. If the roadmap for transition from a non-ISDN environment to an ISDN-enhanced environment is a sensible one, users can begin to enjoy the benefits of ISDN without breaking the bank in the process.

At Motorola Codex, we call these roadmaps "migration strategies." And at the risk of tooting our own horn, we think that we devise excellent migration strategies for companies wanting to get into ISDN. The reason is simple: for more than a quarter of a century, on behalf of businesses around the world, we've been making otherwise uncooperative technologies work together happily.

**At Motorola Codex, we can help you develop an ISDN strategy that makes sense for your business.**

We've been helping companies all over the world build reliable, cost-cutting communications networks. Along the way, we've also built ourselves quite a reputation.

Why is Motorola Codex consistently singled out as a networking leader?

First, it's for the reliability of our products. They *perform*, plain and simple. You won't find another vendor's product line that has more consistently high quality and reliability ratings than ours.

It's also for the range of networking solutions you'll find at Motorola Codex. Because networking is our only business, we're uniquely equipped to design a customized analog, digital, ISDN, or hybrid solution to meet your company's tele- and data communications requirements. We can also provide a network management system to control and maintain your network, once installed. And finally, we can help you make sense out of all the different transmission technologies and products available today, simplifying the complex business of building and maintaining a communications network.

Of course, Motorola Codex is also known for outstanding customer service. Our responsive customer support organization includes networking consultants, applications engineers, and service technicians located around the world.

And as a wholly owned subsidiary of Motorola, Inc., we have all the financial and technological backing of a multibillion dollar electronics leader, including access to the industry's leading semiconductor technology.

That's Motorola Codex in just a few words. But if you have any kind of communications network, we have lots more to talk about. Just return the reply card at the end of this book, or call your Motorola Codex sales representative.

# INDEX